MARC HUNDLEY'S
DICTIONARY

CIRCLE & SQUARE
NEW YORK, NY

Set in Monotype Bembo
Printed on the occasion of the show *Dictionary*
at Art Since the Summer of '69
Printed in New York, NY
Co-published by Circle & Square and Art Since the Summer of '69
ISBN: 978-0-9834024-1-1

The following is a selection of illustrations
from Marc Hundley's dictionary.

acorn

Actaeon

Adam²

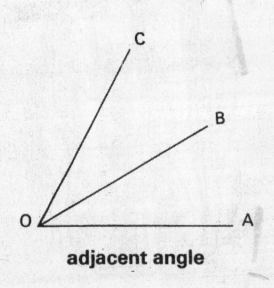

adjacent angle

Adonis[1]

Aeolus

Aesculapius

Agni

alpenstock

anaconda

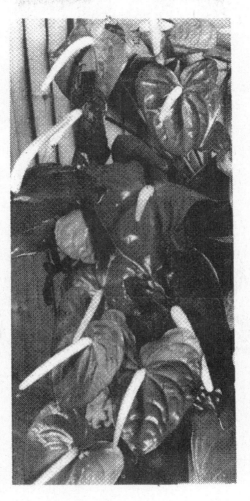

anthurium

Apollo

atrium

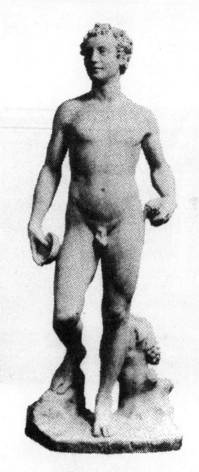

Bacchus

bark

bascule

basketball

beret

Giovanni Bernini

berth

Big Ben

bighorn

boomerang

bowfin

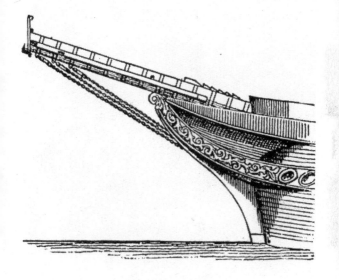

bowsprit

breadfruit

breeches buoy

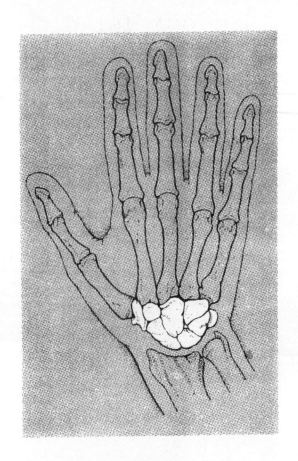

carpus

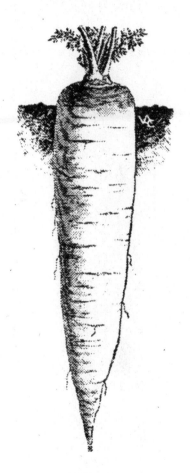

carrot

35

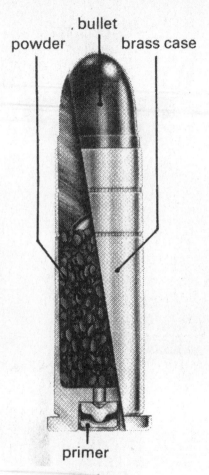

powder   bullet   brass case

primer

cartridge

cattail

John Chapman

clarinet

clitellum

clown

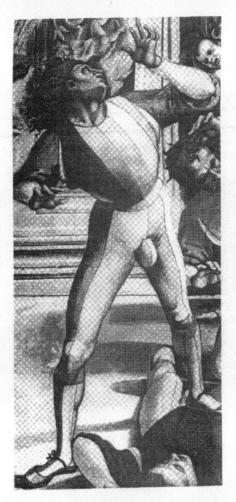

codpiece

abacus
block

capital

shaft

base

column

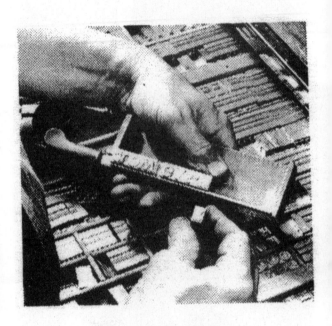

composing stick

control tower

corn[1]

corolla

cot¹

Gustave Courbet

cricket²

crow's-nest

cucumber

Daphne

diamondback

dipper

dirigible

dispenser

Douglas fir

English horn

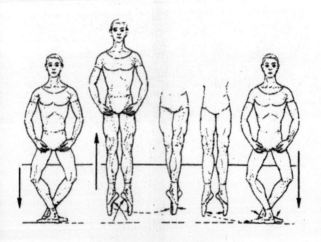

entrechat

fedora

football

footrope

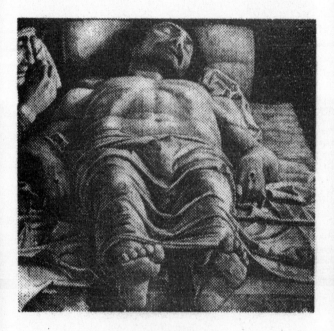

foreshorten

French door

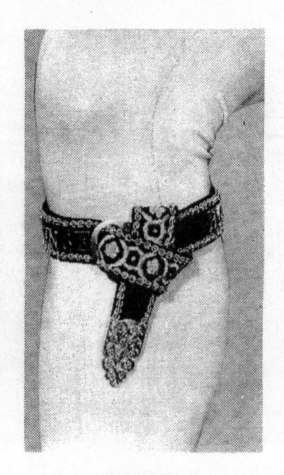

garter

gladiator

havelock

Hercules[1]

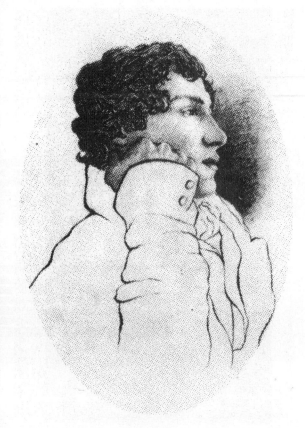

John Keats

kiln

D. H. Lawrence

life jacket

life preserver

lifeboat

lighthouse

lime[1]

lizard

Aristide Maillol

Guglielmo Marconi

Mercury

metope

Michelangelo

moon

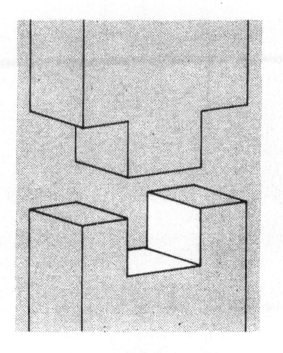

mortise

tongue   soft palate
palatine tonsil   uvula

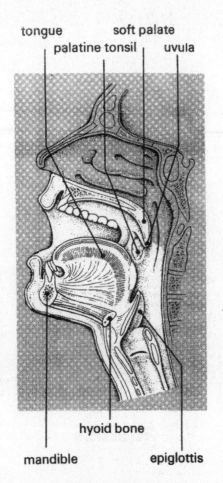

hyoid bone

mandible   epiglottis

mouth

nest

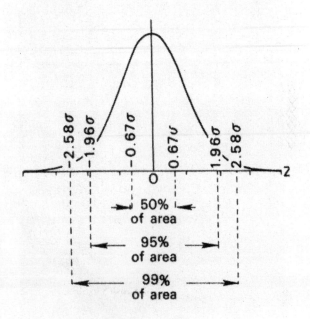

normal distribution

okra

organ-pipe cactus

Orpheus

overalls

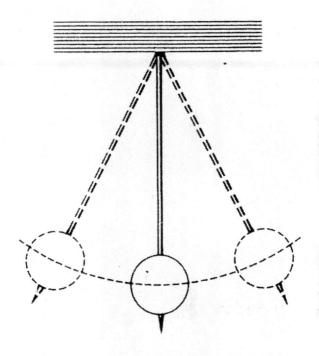

pendulum

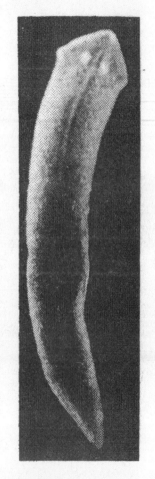

planarian

pole vault

profile

Prometheus

Proteus

puttee

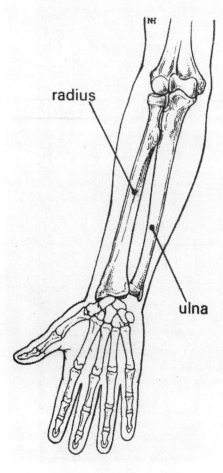

radius

ulna

radius

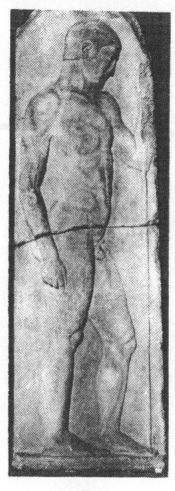

relief

rudder

Rugby football

sawhorse

scuba

scythe

sea anemone

sea cucumber

sentry box

shell

shepherd

silo

Silvanus

Upton Sinclair

soccer

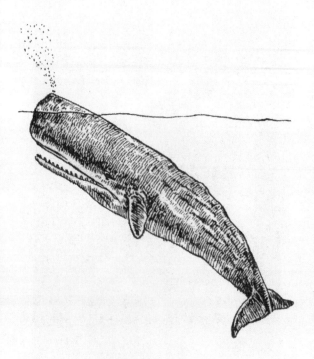

sperm whale

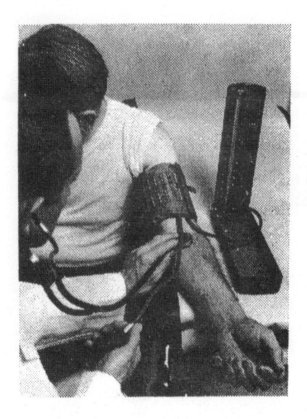

sphygmomanometer

Stetson

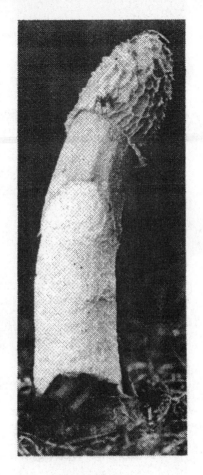

stinkhorn

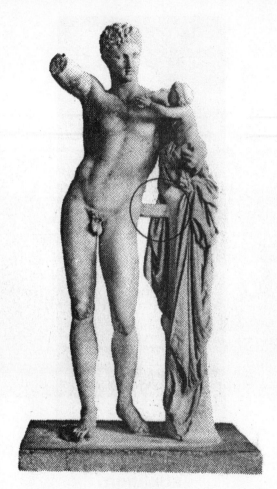

strut

subway

tam-o'-shanter

ten-gallon hat

tent¹

tutu

valance

Van de Graaff generator

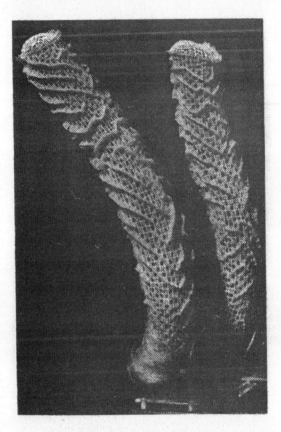

Venus's flower basket

watch cap

weather balloon

wrestling

133

zeppelin

Zeus

zucchini